# what would you ask?
## MARCO POLO

**Anita Ganeri**
Illustrated by Ross Watton

Thameside Press

U.S. publication copyright © 1999 Thameside Press.
International copyright reserved in all countries.
No part of this book may be reproduced in any form
without written permission from the publisher.

Distributed in the United States by
Smart Apple Media
123 South Broad Street
Mankato, Minnesota 56001

Text copyright © Anita Ganeri 1999

Editors: Veronica Ross & Claire Edwards
Designer: Simeen Karim
Illustrator: Ross Watton
Consultant: Hester Collicutt

Printed in China

ISBN: 1-929298-00-5
Library of Congress Catalog Card Number 99-73402

10 9 8 7 6 5 4 3 2 1

# Contents

# What do you do?

"I am an Italian merchant and explorer. I have traveled all over the world."

In 1271 a young Italian, Marco Polo, set out with his father and uncle on an incredible journey. They traveled from their home in Venice to mysterious Cathay, the country we now call China. Cathay was thousands of miles away to the east and far beyond the known world.

It was the adventure of a lifetime. And Marco was just 17 years old. On the way, they crossed high mountain ranges, mighty rivers, and great deserts, which people said were haunted. Finally, in 1275, they reached the fabulous court of the ruler of China—the great Kublai Khan.

Marco wrote about his adventures in a book called *The Travels of Marco Polo—a Description of the World*. The book became a bestseller and inspired many other traders and explorers to follow in Marco's footsteps.

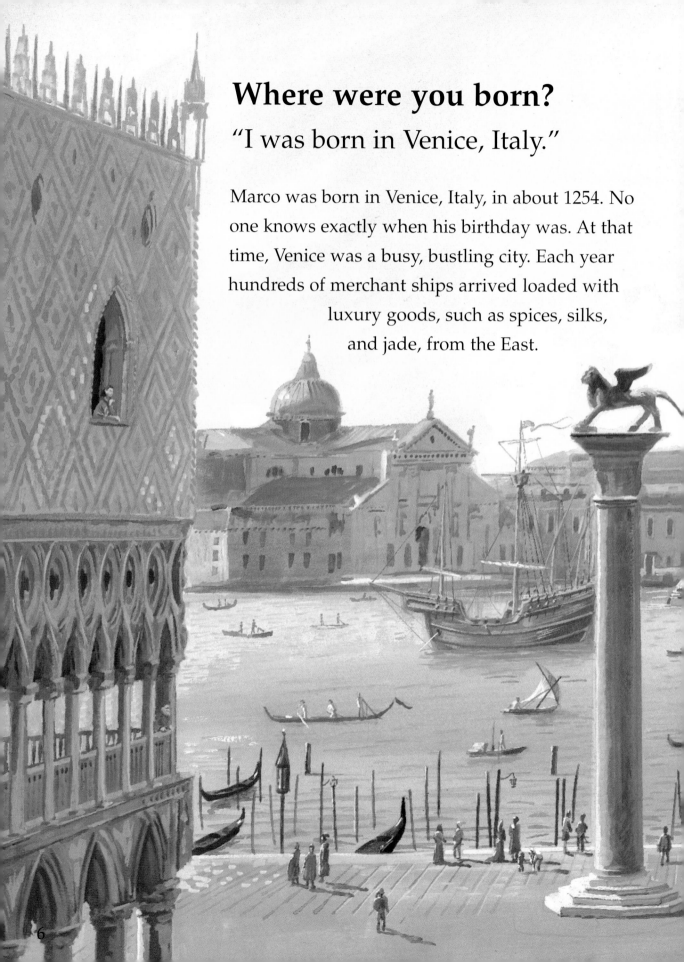

# Where were you born?

## "I was born in Venice, Italy."

Marco was born in Venice, Italy, in about 1254. No one knows exactly when his birthday was. At that time, Venice was a busy, bustling city. Each year hundreds of merchant ships arrived loaded with luxury goods, such as spices, silks, and jade, from the East.

When Marco was about six years old, his father, Niccolo, sailed away to Constantinople. Marco was left at home and did not see his father for nine years. We do not know whether Marco went to school, but he probably learned to read, write and add. Perhaps he also spent his days in the harbor, dreaming of the exotic places his father was visiting.

Just before Marco's sixteenth birthday, his mother got sick and died. Soon afterward, his father came home to Venice. But he did not stay for very long.

# What did your family do?

## "My father and uncle bought and sold goods from the Far East."

Marco's father, Niccolo, and his uncle, Maffeo, were wealthy Venetian merchants. They were very adventurous, traveling far and wide to trade. But traveling was dangerous, with many robbers and bandits hiding along the way.

In 1260, the Polos set off for the city of Constantinople and then on to China and the city of Shangdu, the capital of the Mongol Empire. Kublai Khan welcomed them warmly, and the three men became good friends. When the time came for Niccolo and Maffeo to leave, Kublai Khan made them promise that one day they would return to China.

Although Kublai Khan was a Buddhist, he was very interested in other religions. He gave the Polos a message for the Pope, asking him to send a hundred priests who could perform magic tricks. He also told the Polos to bring some oil from the sacred lamp that burned in the Holy Sepulcher in Jerusalem.

# How old were you when you set off on your travels?

"I was 17 years old. It was the start of a great adventure."

Niccolo and Maffeo spent fewer than two years in Venice before they were off on their travels again. This time, they took young Marco with them. Little did he know that he would not be home for another 20 years.

In 1271, the Polos traveled to Jerusalem to collect the holy oil for Kublai Khan. They also met the Pope, who gave them gifts for the Great Khan and sent two priests to travel with them back to China. But the priests ran away, leaving the Polos to continue alone.

For most of the journey, the Polos followed a route called the Silk Road. The road was difficult and dangerous, but Kublai Khan had given the Polos special gold tablets, or passes, to carry with them. These showed that they had his permission to travel in safety. The Polos needed these tablets. No one had ever traveled the whole length of the Silk Road before—no one had dared.

# How long did the journey take?

"A very long time! We finally reached Kublai Khan's palace three and a half years later."

On their journey, the Polos crossed vast deserts and some of the highest mountains in the world. They had many narrow escapes from danger. Bandits tried to rob them, and, once, when Marco got sick, their journey was delayed for a whole year. They traveled on foot, on horseback, and by donkey and mule. Often, they joined up with other riders to form a caravan. It was too risky to travel alone.

Marco made notes of the sights he saw. In Baku, he was fascinated by a fountain of oil which gushed from the ground day and night. Local people burned the oil in lamps. Marco was also interested in the many different people he met and in their crafts, jobs, customs, and ways of life. Some of them seemed very weird and wonderful to him.

At last, in May 1275, the Polos reached China and the court of Kublai Khan. Here they gave him the letter and gifts from the Pope, and the holy oil from Jerusalem.

# What was your scariest moment?

"It was when we crossed the Gobi Desert.
That was really frightening."

The Polos crossed Persia and climbed up into Afghanistan, over
the towering Hindu Kush and Pamir mountains. They traveled
along the edge of the Takla Makan Desert and into the Gobi Desert.
Many travelers believed the desert was haunted.

Day and night, the Polos heard ghostly voices and noises like drum beats. The voices seemed to be trying to trick them. If they followed the voices and strayed from the path, they would soon be hopelessly lost in the desert. In fact, the sounds were probably made by the rocks shrinking in the cold night, after the heat of the day.

# What did you do in China?

## "I worked as an ambassador for Kublai Khan, traveling all over China."

When the Polos reached Kublai Khan's court, the emperor was delighted to see them. Marco learned how to speak and write the Mongol language and became one of the Great Khan's most trusted ambassadors. He was sent to distant parts of the empire and beyond to Burma. Kublai Khan looked forward to Marco's return and to his news of all the unusual things he had seen on his travels.

Kublai Khan ruled China from two palaces—his summer palace in Shangdu and his winter palace in Cambaluc. Marco was dazzled by their splendor. The summer palace was built from stone and marble, and its rooms were decorated with paintings of birds, trees, and flowers. The palace had a vast walled garden, where the emperor hunted with falcons and leopards. In the middle, there was a summer house made from bamboo reeds and bright silks, where the emperor spent the hottest days.

# What did you like best about China?

"I saw so many amazing places and things, it is difficult to pick just one."

In China, Marco saw many strange and wonderful things. He was especially interested in Chinese money. The Chinese used paper money, which Marco had never seen before. Printed paper bills were stamped with their value in bronze, silver, or gold. The Chinese used the money to buy goods in the local markets.

In fact, printing, paper, and paper money were all invented in China. These inventions spread from China to the rest of the world. Marco was also amazed by "black stones" that burned like wood. These burning stones were actually coal fires. Marco later described how people used the fires to heat their bath water. It was a good thing that there was so much coal because people seemed to bathe a lot—much more than in Venice!

But out of all the things Marco saw and all the places he visited, one place stood out above the rest—the fantastic city of Kinsai.

# What was the most exciting place you visited?

## "Oh, it was definitely the city of Kinsai."

The place that impressed Marco most was Kinsai, in the east of China. In his book, he describes it as "the most majestic and wealthy city in the world." Its name meant "the city of Heaven." Located between a great lake and river, Kinsai was criss-crossed with canals and bridges, just like Venice.

In each of its main squares there were ten markets, where you could buy anything from pepper to pearls. On market days, each square was packed with thousands of townspeople.

For Marco, the nicest part of the city was the lake, surrounded by trees and temples. In the middle of the lake, there were two islands, and each island had a pavilion. These were used for weddings and parties—sometimes a hundred parties would be going on at once.

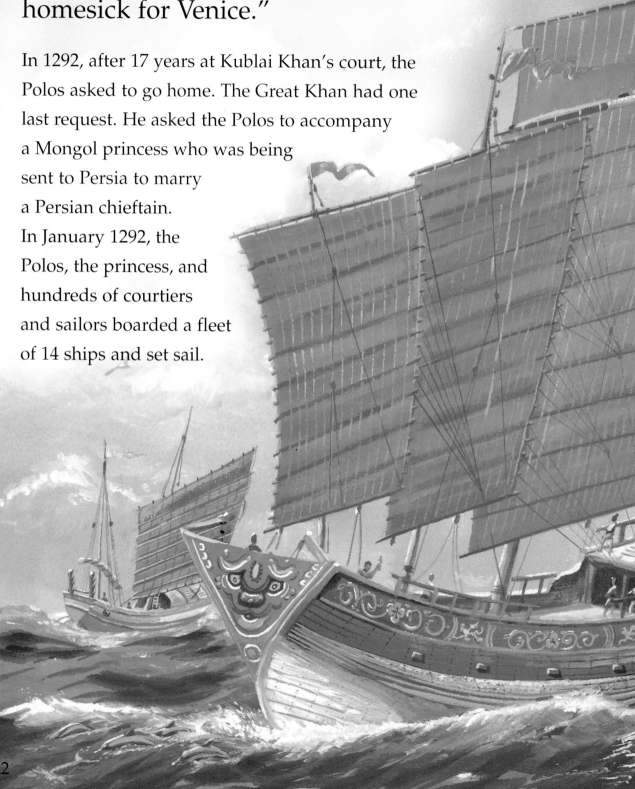

# Why did you leave China?

## "My father and uncle were homesick for Venice."

In 1292, after 17 years at Kublai Khan's court, the Polos asked to go home. The Great Khan had one last request. He asked the Polos to accompany a Mongol princess who was being sent to Persia to marry a Persian chieftain. In January 1292, the Polos, the princess, and hundreds of courtiers and sailors boarded a fleet of 14 ships and set sail.

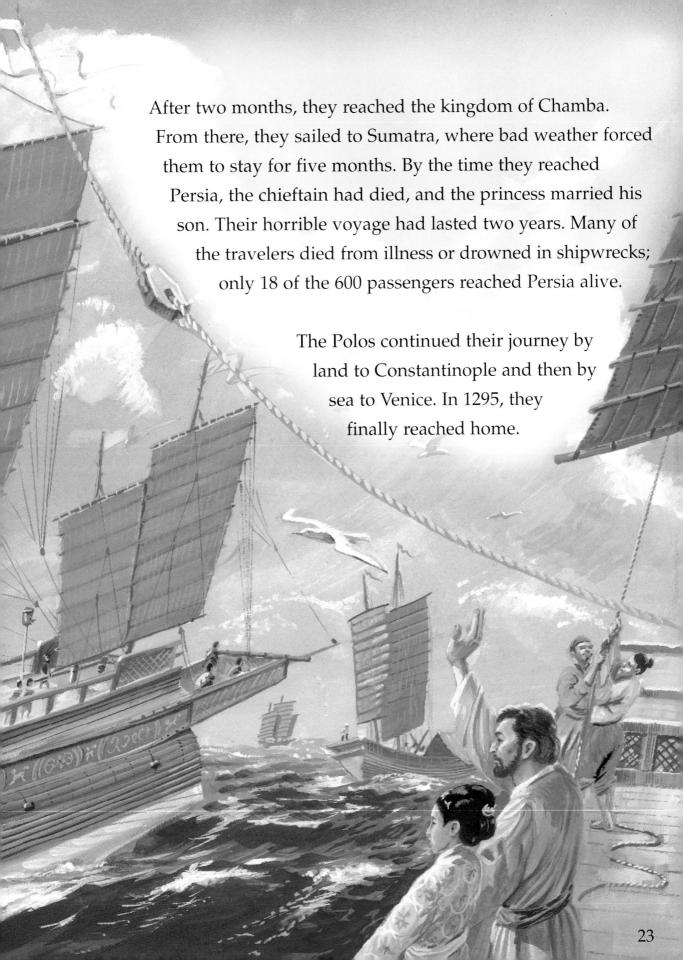

After two months, they reached the kingdom of Chamba. From there, they sailed to Sumatra, where bad weather forced them to stay for five months. By the time they reached Persia, the chieftain had died, and the princess married his son. Their horrible voyage had lasted two years. Many of the travelers died from illness or drowned in shipwrecks; only 18 of the 600 passengers reached Persia alive.

The Polos continued their journey by land to Constantinople and then by sea to Venice. In 1295, they finally reached home.

# What happened when you got home?
## "Unfortunately, I ended up in prison!"

The Polos' arrival in Venice caused a huge stir. Many of their friends and relations thought they had died a long time ago and were amazed to see them alive and well. They were even more stunned to see that the Polos' clothes were stuffed with precious jewels.

Marco was now about 40 years old. But his new, more settled life at home did not last long.

Within three years of his return, Venice
was at war with the city of Genoa,
fighting for control of the best trade
routes. Marco was captured during a
battle at sea and was locked up in prison
in Genoa. While Marco was there, he met
a fellow prisoner called Rustichello.
To pass the long days, Marco began
to tell Rustichello the story of his life.

# Did you write about your travels?

"Yes, I wrote a book called *The Travels of Marco Polo*."

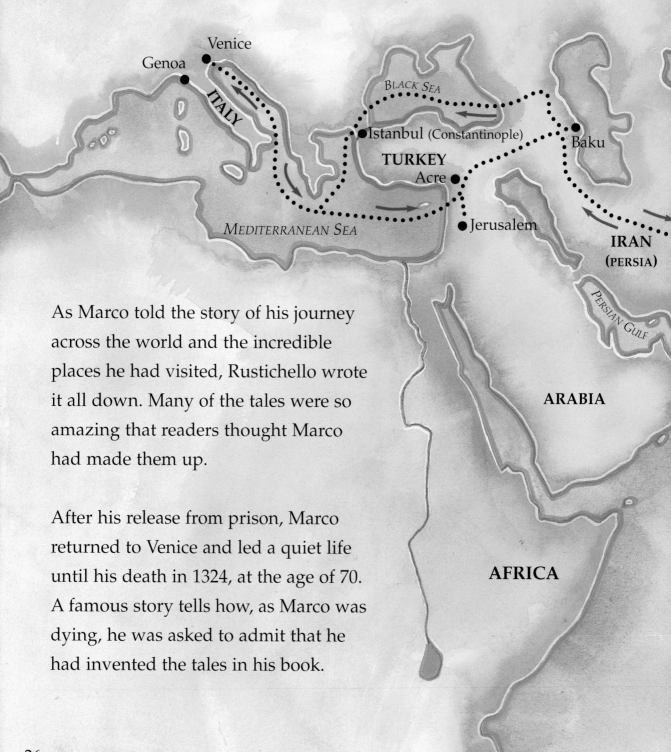

As Marco told the story of his journey across the world and the incredible places he had visited, Rustichello wrote it all down. Many of the tales were so amazing that readers thought Marco had made them up.

After his release from prison, Marco returned to Venice and led a quiet life until his death in 1324, at the age of 70. A famous story tells how, as Marco was dying, he was asked to admit that he had invented the tales in his book.

Marco answered that he had told barely half of what he had seen. Today, we know that much of what Marco Polo described really was the truth. His amazing journey opened up a new world to readers and travelers alike.

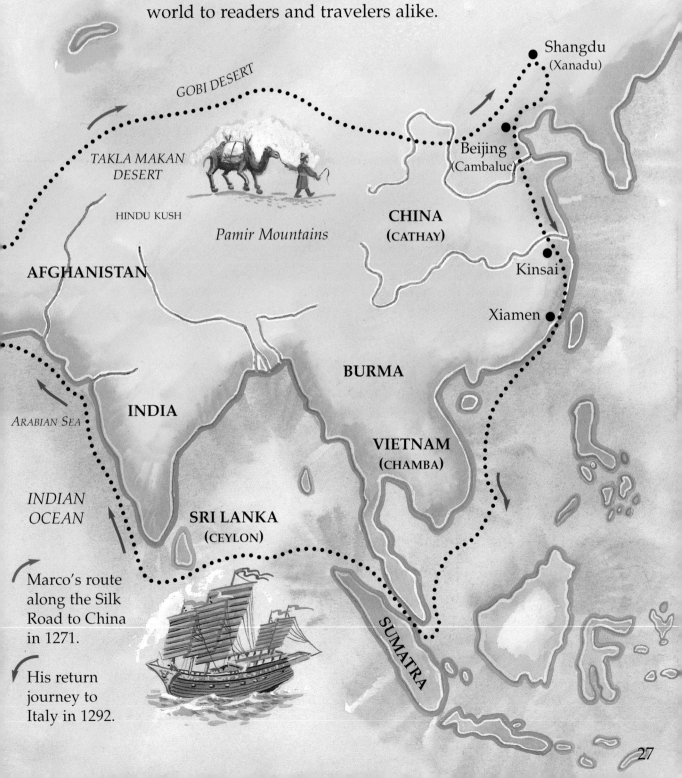

GOBI DESERT

Shangdu (Xanadu)

TAKLA MAKAN DESERT

HINDU KUSH

Pamir Mountains

Beijing (Cambaluc)

CHINA (CATHAY)

AFGHANISTAN

Kinsai

Xiamen

ARABIAN SEA

INDIA

BURMA

INDIAN OCEAN

VIETNAM (CHAMBA)

SRI LANKA (CEYLON)

SUMATRA

Marco's route along the Silk Road to China in 1271.

His return journey to Italy in 1292.

# Some important dates

**1251** Kublai Khan becomes Mongol emperor. He rules over a huge empire, stretching from eastern Europe to India and China.

**1254** Marco Polo is born in Venice, Italy, to a wealthy merchant family.

**1260** Marco's father, Niccolo, and uncle, Maffeo, leave Venice on their first journey to China. Marco is just six years old when he says goodbye to his father.

**1269** Marco's mother gets sick and dies. Shortly afterward, Niccolo and Maffeo return from the East.

**1271** Aged 17, Marco sets out with his father and uncle to travel from Venice to China. They travel most of the way on land, on the Silk Road.

**1275** In May, the Polos reach Kublai Khan's court. They stay there for 17 years. During this time, Marco travels all over China, and beyond, on official business for the emperor.

**1279** The Mongols conquer southern China. Kublai Khan is recognized as ruler of all China.

**1292** The Polos leave China for home. They escort a Mongol princess to Persia, then continue their journey back to Europe.

**1295** The Polos return to Venice after being away for 20 years. Kublai Khan dies. The Mongol empire lasts for another 70 years, but it is never as strong again.

**1298** During a sea battle, Marco is captured by the Genoese and put in prison. He tells his life story to another prisoner, Rustichello. Rustichello writes it down as a book called *The Travels of Marco Polo*. People nickname the book *Il Milione* (*The Million*) to give the idea that Marco has made the tales up, or at least exaggerated. The book becomes a bestseller.

**1299** Peace is declared between Venice and Genoa, and Marco is released from jail.

**1324** On January 8, Marco dies in Venice, aged 70.

**1350** The Silk Road is closed because it has become too dangerous.

**1368** In China, the Mongols are overthrown. They are replaced by the Chinese Ming dynasty (ruling family), which rules until 1644.

**1477** The first printed version of *The Travels* is produced in Germany. Before this, copies were written out by hand.

**1492** Christopher Columbus sails from Spain to America, taking a copy of Marco Polo's *Travels* with him.

# Glossary

**ambassador** An official who represents his or her country in another place.

**bamboo** A giant type of grass grown in China. It was used to make everything from baskets to the roofs of houses, and as food for animals.

**bandit** A robber who usually belonged to a gang.

**Buddhist** Someone who follows the teachings of Siddhartha Gautama, a prince who became the Buddha when he realized the truth about life. He lived in India in about the sixth century B.C.

**caravan** A group of people and animals traveling together, often carrying goods for trade. The Polos probably traveled as part of a camel caravan along the Silk Road.

**chieftain** The leader of a tribe or group of people in one area.

**Christopher Columbus** (1451–1506) An Italian-born Spanish explorer, who is said to have been the first European to land in America. Columbus always believed that he had landed in Asia.

**courtiers** People who work in a ruler's court.

**customs** The usual ways in which a country's people do things, such as cook their food, hold festivals, and dress.

**empire** A large area, often made up of several countries, which is ruled by a powerful leader, called an emperor or an empress.

**exotic** Another word for strange or unusual. It also means something that comes from a foreign country.

**haunted** Visited by ghosts or spirits. People thought the Gobi Desert was haunted by evil spirits.

**Holy Sepulcher** The tomb in which Jesus Christ is said to have been buried in Jerusalem.

**jade** A hard, green stone that is used for jewelry and decoration. Jade can also be blue or white.

**khan** The Mongol word for leader.

**kingdom** A country that is ruled by a king or queen.

**marble** A type of stone used for building and sculpture.

**merchant** Someone who makes a living by buying and selling goods, often from other countries. A merchant is also called a trader. Marco Polo came from a rich merchant family.

**Mongols** People from Central Asia who conquered a huge empire. Their leader was Kublai Khan.

**pavilion** A decorated building, usually with open sides.

**Pope** The leader, or head, of the Roman Catholic Church.

**sacred** Another word for holy.

**Silk Road** This was one of the oldest trading routes between Europe and China. Chinese merchants sent spices and silk westward to Europe in return for gold, silver, and jewels.

# Index